YOU WERE BORN ON YOUR
VERY FIRST BIRTHDAY

Linda Walvoord Girard   *pictures by* Christa Kieffer

ALBERT WHITMAN & COMPANY, NILES, ILLINOIS

Library of Congress Cataloging in Publication Data

Girard, Linda Walvoord.
   You were born on your very first birthday.

   (Concept Book. Level 1)
   Summary: Describes the life of a tiny baby in his
safe, warm, floating place during the nine months
before he is born.
   [1. Fetus—Fiction. 2. Babies—Fiction] I. Kieffer,
Christa, ill. II. Title. III. Series.
PZ7.G43953Yo 1983   [E]   82-13700
ISBN 0-8075-9455-5

The text of this book is set in sixteen point Caslon 540.

For Aaron

Before you were born
you had a special place
where you curled up inside your mommy.
For nine months
while the weather and the seasons changed outside
and the wind blew in the trees
it was always exactly the same every day
in your place. Safe. Floating. Warm.

You grew there, slept,
wiggled, and waited for your birthday.
Only you didn't know what in the world
a birthday was—or what cake is,
or a bed, or a mom and dad, or morning,
or a room of toys.

You didn't know anything, in fact,
except how warm it was sleeping
all curled up.

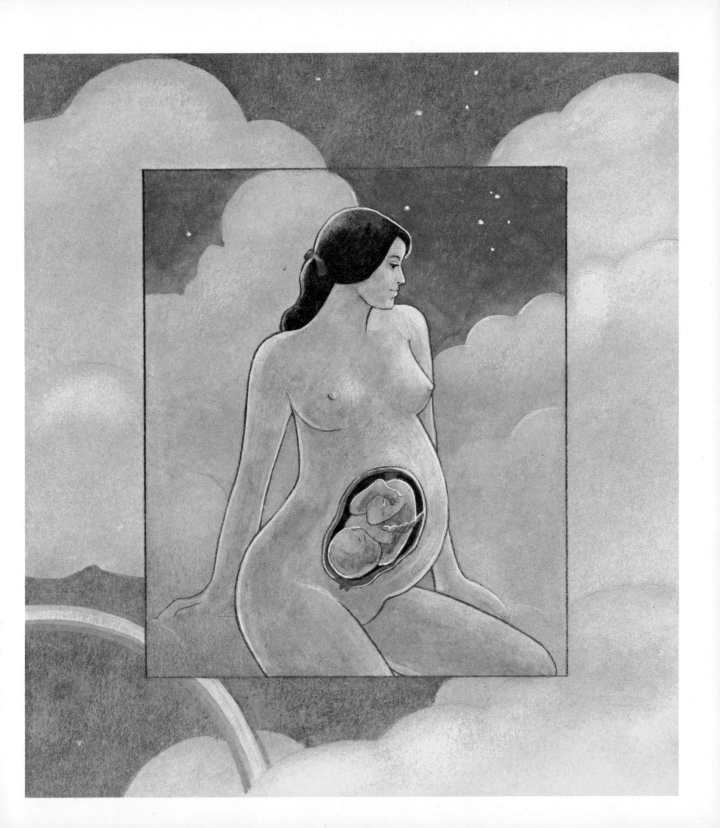

First you were smaller than a pea.

You grew. Pretty soon you were the size
your thumb is now. You kept growing.

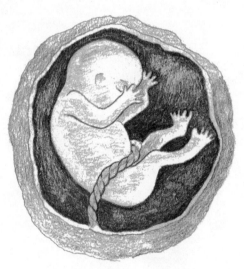

Soon you were the size of your mommy's hand.
The size of a puppy.
All the while you were growing, your place
was growing too, to make room for you.

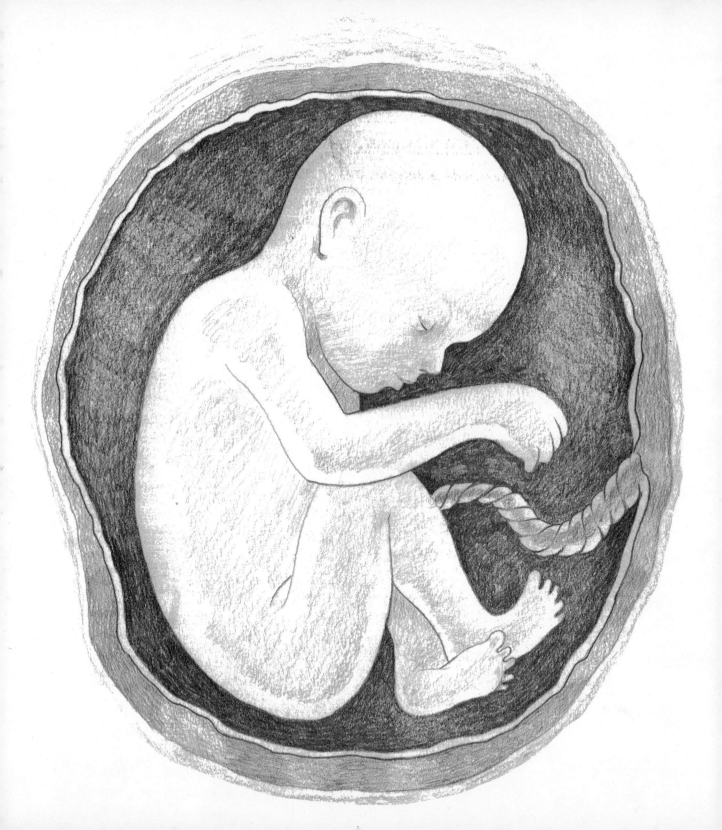

And all that time, what could you do?
You could suck your thumb.
You could feel your mother's heart beat—*thump, thump.*
You could wiggle your feet. Far off, out in the world,
you could hear things roar or rattle
as your mommy walked down the street.

If she went to a symphony concert,
you could feel the big bass drum go
thum, *thum*, *thum*.
Every time it thummed, you moved.

And you could feel your mommy
talking sometimes. You didn't know words
or what she was saying. *Hmmmmm.*
Pppppppp. Rap-a-tap. Mmmmmmmnk. Hmmmmm.
That's how it sounded, watery and hummy,
no matter what she was saying.
Her words hummed in your bones.

Sometimes you'd give your mom a little kick, just for fun.
One time you got the hiccups.
That was a bumpy day for everyone.

As you grew bigger, sometimes you felt
a little too warm. A little cramped.
You wanted something. What?
You moved your arms. You stretched.
You wiggled your feet. Nope,
that wasn't quite what you wanted.
Something.

Did you want the world—
green and red and purple, with wind
and trees and bikes and chocolate
and balloons? And Mom and Dad?

How could you know what you wanted?

"Hush," your mom said to you
sometimes at night. "Go to sleep."
But how did you know what she said?
You didn't even know it was night.

You dreamed about the sounds.
Rap-a-tap. Mmmmmmmnk. Pppppll.
Dimly you felt something was going to happen.
Soon. You grew very quiet.
Something inside you knew you were ready.
Your eyes were ready to see.
Your voice was ready to grunt, or howl, or coo.
Your stomach was ready for some new food.

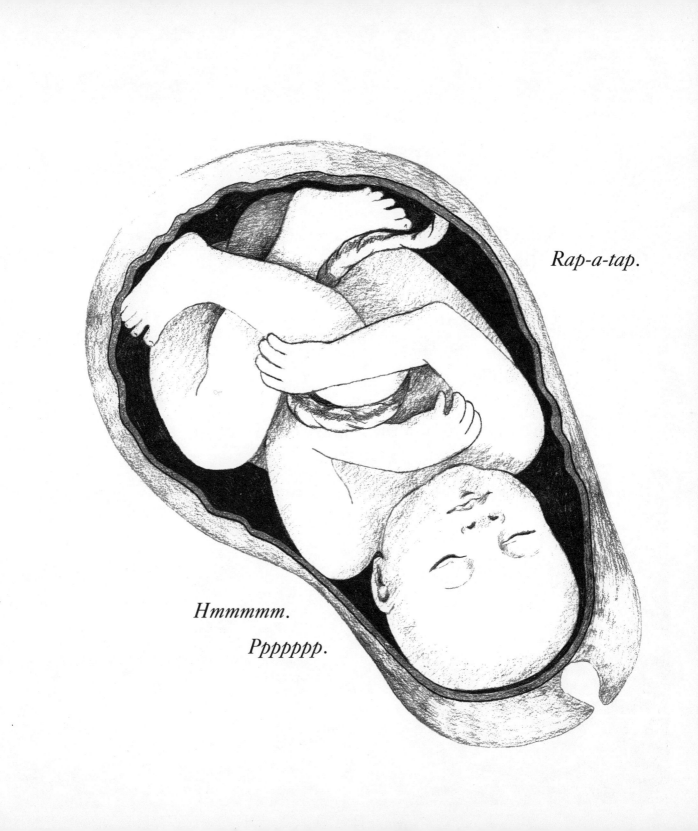

Rap-a-tap.

Hmmmm.

Pppppppp.

So one day, one special day—
there was a twitch. Twitch. Nudge.
Nudge. Nudge.
Something inside you thought, oh.
Is this it? Is this what I'm waiting for?
You kept very still.
Hmmmm. And then—
you felt a squeeze
like a hug.
Thump. Heave. Hmph.
One hug after another, bigger and bigger.

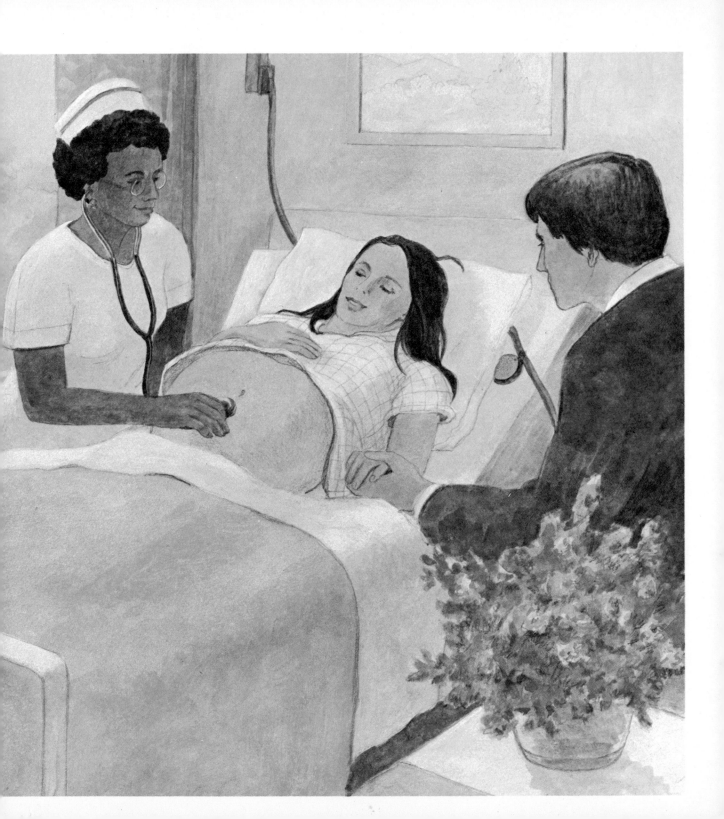

Giant hugs. Oh boy shove ooph
it's tight in here—
I'm turning
where am I going
Oh-o-o-o-o-oh! Wow!

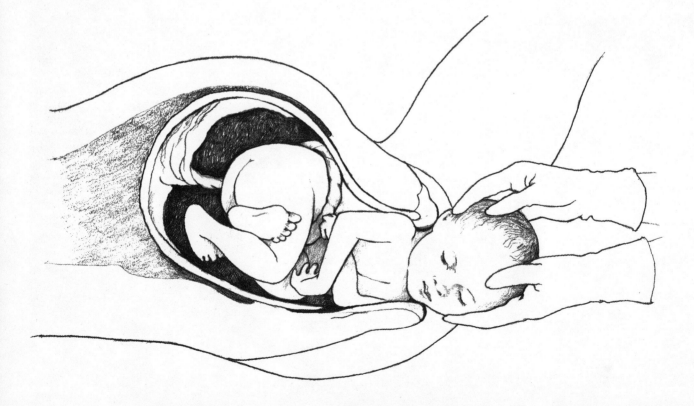

Out you came
along a narrow path
that was opening wider and wider
a special pathway only for you
out of your mother's body.
Your mother helped give you a push.
Your daddy was waiting.
It was a very tight squeeze.
But you made it.

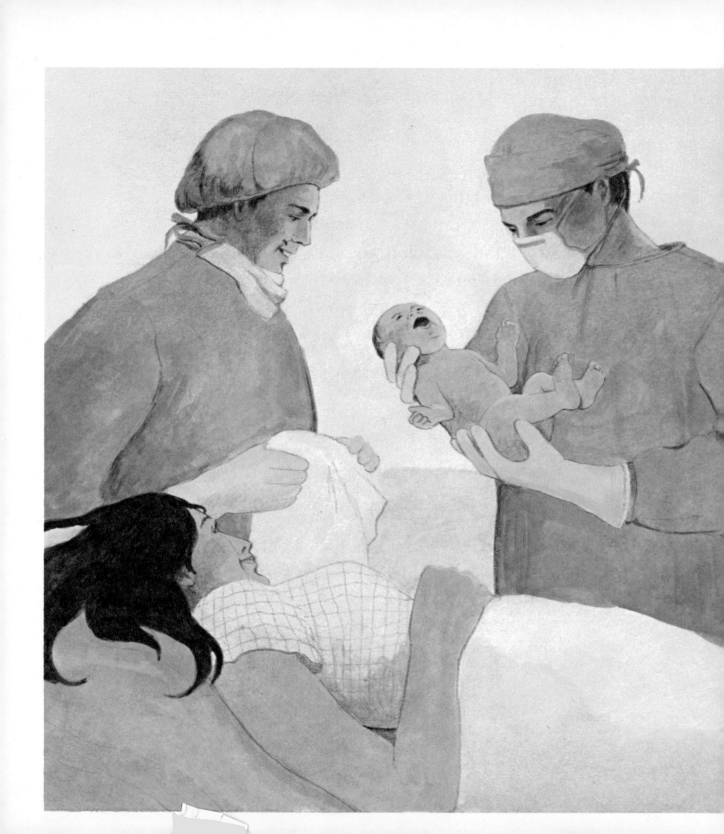

And then—there you were!
There was the world—lights!
Sounds! Action!
Some hands cuddled you and wrapped you
in a soft blanket. You heard yourself crying.
What's *that* loud noise? you might have thought.

At that moment, your mom was smiling a giant smile.
She thought, if this baby can make all that noise,
this baby must be just fine!
Your mom and dad didn't even know you yet,
but they loved you.
They looked into your blurry eyes.
You stared at them as if to say,
"Well—here I am!"
And their eyes got all blurry, too, and they said,
"Oh, it's your birthday!" and "Oh!
You're beautiful!"

Everybody felt all blurry and warm and you did, too.